PANAMA CANAL

HISTORY FOR KIDS

ARCHITECTURE, PURPOSE & DESIGN
TIMELINES OF HISTORY FOR KIDS
6TH GRADE SOCIAL STUDIES

BABY PROFESSOR

EDUCATION KIDS

Speedy Publishing LLC

40 E. Main St. #1156

Newark, DE 19711

www.speedypublishing.com

Copyright 2018

In this book, we're going to talk about the history of the Panama Canal. So, let's get right to it!

B uilt by thousands of men, the Panama Canal is a structure that's a marvel of engineering. Before the canal was built, in order for a ship to travel from the Atlantic Ocean to the Pacific Ocean, it had to travel all the way south to the tip of South America.

ISTHMUS OF DARIEN

The Panama Canal provided a shortcut across the Isthmus of Panama. This region, previously called the Isthmus of Darien, is a narrow piece of land. The Caribbean Sea is to the east of it and to its west is the Pacific Ocean.

WHEN WAS THE PANAMA CANAL BUILT?

The construction work to build the canal was started in 1881. At the beginning, the French were in charge but they began to run into problems. Workers were dying of disease and there were problems with the complicated construction necessary to build the canal. The French abandoned the project and in 1904, the United States took over. After more than a decade of hard labor, the canal was opened for ships to pass through in the month of August in 1914.

PANAMA CANAL CONSTRUCTION SHOWING WORKERS DRILLING HOLES

MAP OF PANAMA

WHY CHOOSE PANAMA FOR THIS CANAL?

If you look at a globe, you'll easily see why the country of Panama and specifically the Isthmus of Panama was picked for this project. It's the narrowest strip of land that divides the two large oceans. It was the most logical spot to construct a passageway connecting the two waterways. Despite the fact that the land there wasn't a very large strip, the project was still incredibly difficult.

WHY WAS THE PANAMA CANAL BUILT?

Before the canal was constructed, a trip from the city of New York to the city of San Francisco would have taken a ship about 5 months from start to destination.

PANAMA CANAL

The ship would have to travel about 8,000 miles more than the distance if passing through the canal. The Panama Canal decreased the distance for shipping thereby saving time and money for shipping companies. When the canal opened, it was a huge boost to the worldwide economy.

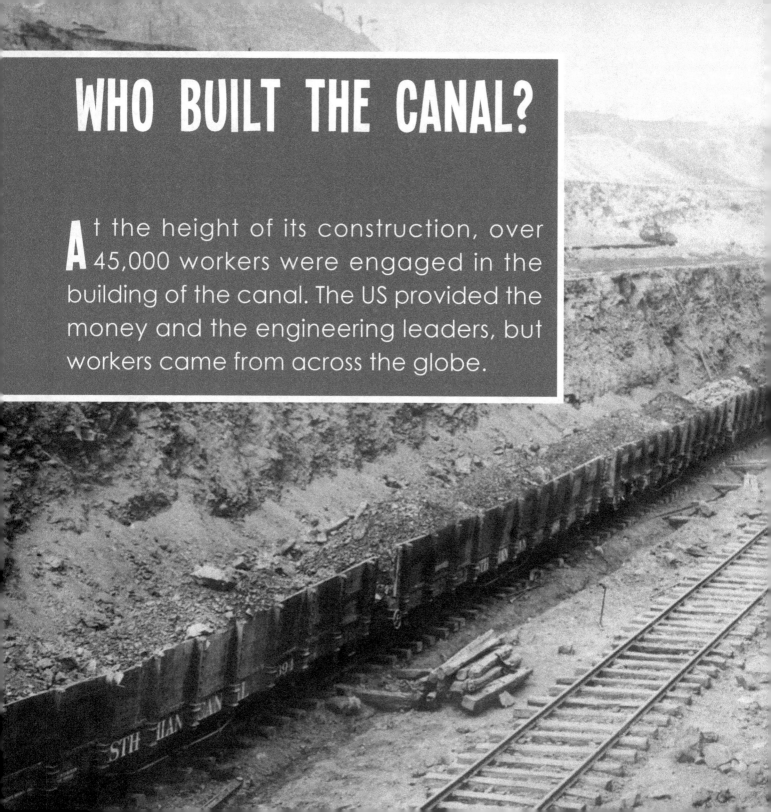

WHO BUILT THE CANAL?

At the height of its construction, over 45,000 workers were engaged in the building of the canal. The US provided the money and the engineering leaders, but workers came from across the globe.

Three leaders who were influential in the project were:

JOHN STEVENS

He was the engineer who persuaded President Teddy Roosevelt that the canal would need to be elevated.

WILLIAM GORGAS

He was the manager who devised ways to kill mosquitoes so the workers wouldn't die from disease.

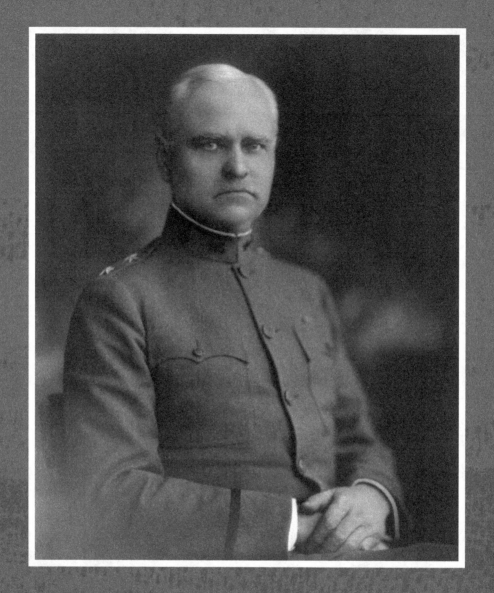

GEORGE GOETHALS

He was the leader of the construction project beginning in 1907.

THE CONSTRUCTION OF THE CANAL

The leaders and workers had to overcome many problems to build the canal. There were mosquito-borne diseases and the ever-present threat of snakes and scorpions.

Dangerous mudslides happened during the construction process, especially during the Culebra Cut phase of the construction. In addition, the living conditions were deplorable causing the workers to become weak and ill. Despite all these problems, the canal was eventually built and showed some of the most innovative engineering techniques available at the time.

PANAMA CANAL

THE GATES AT THE GATUN LOCKS ON THE PANAMA CANAL

The construction took place in three different phases:

CONSTRUCTING THE LOCKS

The locks are chambers within the canal. The locks are immense with a width of 110 feet and a length of 1,050 feet. Their walls are huge and were constructed from concrete. The gates are made of steel. They are 60 feet in height and their thickness is 6 feet. The locks are used to elevate the water level under the ships.

EXCAVATING THE CULEBRA CUT

This portion of the canal required workers to dig through Panama's mountains. There were landslides and large sections of falling rock, which made this portion of the project the most hazardous.

THE SHIP IS PASSING THE CUCARACHA SLIDE, IN THE CULEBRA CUT.

CONSTRUCTING THE DAM AT GATUN RIVER

In order for the canal to work as intended, the designers created an artificial lake in the middle of the country. They built an enormous dam located at Gatun River and named the resulting lake, Gatun Lake.

GATUN LAKE

PANAMA CANAL GATEWAY SYSTEM

HOW DOES THE CANAL WORK?

The canal is 48 miles in length. The height of the water in the two oceans isn't the same. The Pacific Ocean is higher than the Atlantic Ocean is. To solve this problem there are locks on each side of the canal. These locks allow the ships to be raised or lowered depending on whether they are traveling from east to west or vice versa. This adjustment of the water level makes it possible for ships to travel through the canal and over to the other ocean. No matter what the size of the ship is, the process is the same.

An operator closes the locks and then releases water to raise the height of the water under the ship. The ship is held in position with trains called mules at its sides. The ship is attached to the mules with cables to keep it steady as it goes through. It takes 8-10 hours for an individual ship to pass through from where one ocean ends to where the other begins, but that day saves the ship months of travel time.

THE PANAMA CANAL, WHICH CONNECTS THE ATLANTIC OCEAN TO THE PACIFIC OCEAN

THE PROCESS OF TRAVELING FROM THE ATLANTIC TO THE PACIFIC

Here are the typical steps that occur when a ship is traveling from the Atlantic Ocean to the Pacific Ocean through the canal.

The ship enters the chamber at Gatun Locks, which is at sea level on the Atlantic side. The huge doors are closed so that water will stay in the chamber. The lockmaster opens the valves. This action allows water to flow in from pipes underground. The water is coming from a second chamber next to the chamber where the ship is located. This second chamber has water at a height of 28 feet over sea level.

GATUN LOCKS

PANAMA CANAL, INSIDE THE LOCK.

No water pumps are used to raise the height of the water in the ship's chamber. Instead, it's just the natural forces of gravity at work. The water stops flowing when the water level between the two chambers is the same.

THE SECOND LOCK OF THE PANAMA CANAL FROM THE PACIFIC OCEAN.

After the water levels are equalized, the lockmaster closes the water valves and opens the watertight doors to the second of the chambers. The ship travels into the second lock chamber, where the same process is repeated. When the water levels are equalized this second time, it will be released into the third chamber. After this process, the ship is at the same level as Gatun Lake. When the final valve is closed and the watertight doors are opened, the ship has been elevated to a level of 85 feet over sea level.

Next, the ship travels through the narrow passageway through the Culebra Cut and onward to Gatun Lake. After crossing the lake, the ship passes through several additional locks to lower it to the Pacific Ocean. Then, it goes out to the open ocean to continue on its journey.

Ships traveling from the Pacific to the Atlantic follow the opposite process as the water level is lowered in stages. Since the canal opened, over 10 million ships have gone through its locks.

THE FIRST LOCK OF THE PANAMA CANAL FROM THE PACIFIC OCEAN.

TODAY AT THE PANAMA CANAL

The country of Panama was given control over the canal in 1999. The canal is still crucial to importing and exporting today. Over 12,000 cargo ships travel via the canal annually. Over 200,000,000 tons of goods are shipped through the canal every year. The canal also employs over 9,000 citizens.

LARGE CARGO SHIPS WAITING AT GATUN LAKE
TO PASS THROUGH PANAMA CANAL

THIRD SET OF LOCKS CONSTRUCTION SITE.

FASCINATING FACTS ABOUT THE PANAMA CANAL

The total budget for the canal was over $370 million. Today, that would be more than $8 billion.

Although the canal saves shipping companies millions of dollars, it still costs between $50,000 and $300,000 for the canal tolls per ship. However, that's not a high cost when you consider the cost of traveling for months all the way around the tip of South America.

PANAMA

A STEAM SHOVEL LOADS EXCAVATED ROCKS INTO RAILROADS CARS AT GATUN DAM SITE

Unfortunately, the construction of the canal took a huge toll when it came to the lives of the workers. Over 20 thousand died during the French phase of the project and another 5,600 during the United States phase.

HISTORICAL TIMELINE FOR THE PANAMA CANAL

Here are some of the major events in the history of the canal.

1850—The city of Colón is established at the Isthmus of Panama as a passageway for people traveling to the California Gold Rush.

1855—A railroad was built in Panama by the United States.

1880—United States President Rutherford B. Hayes states that the US will be in charge of any canal constructed in Panama.

1903—The country of Panama became independent from the country of Columbia. The United States bought the rights from France to build the canal.

SKYLINE OF PANAMA CITY WITH PANAMIANAN FLAG.

CONSTRUCTION SHOWING MASSIVE LOCKS BEFORE THE GATES WERE INSTALLED.

1904—Construction of the canal begins.

1914—Construction is complete and the United States declares the Panama Canal to be a neutral zone.

SUMMARY

After the French failed to build a canal at the Isthmus of Panama, the United States took over. It took a decade of work, millions of dollars, and over 45 thousand workers from across the globe, but the canal was eventually finished. Since then, the Panama Canal has allowed ships to take a shortcut from the Atlantic to the Pacific. The time and cost savings have more than paid for the budget spent to build the canal.

CARGO SHIPS PASSING THROUGH GATUN LOCKS ON THE ATLANTIC SIDE OF THE PANAMA CANAL.

Awesome! Now that you've read about the history of the Panama Canal, you may want to read about another engineering marvel in the Baby Professor book, Interesting Facts about the Empire State Building - Engineering Book for Boys | Children's Engineering Books.

Visit

BABY PROFESSOR
EDUCATION KIDS

www.BabyProfessorBooks.com

to download Free Baby Professor eBooks
and view our catalog of new and exciting
Children's Books

CPSIA information can be obtained
at www.ICGtesting.com
Printed in the USA
BVHW060042220722
642529BV00008B/222